Alfie's Feet

Also by Shirley Hughes
ALFIE GETS IN FIRST

For

Edward and Catherine

JE
May 12, 1983

Library of Congress Cataloging in Publication Data
Hughes, Shirley.
  Alfie's feet.
  Summary: Alfie is proud of being able to put his
lovely new boots on by himself but wonders why
they feel funny.
  [1. Shoes and boots—Fiction. 2. Left and
right—Fiction] I. Title.
PZ7.H87395Am 1983   [E]   82-13012
ISBN 0-688-01658-8
ISBN 0-688-01660-X (lib. bdg.)

Alfie's Feet

Shirley Hughes

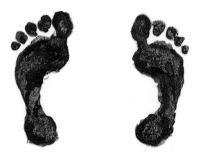

Lothrop, Lee & Shepard Books
New York

This little pig went to market,

This little pig stayed at home,

This little pig had roast beef,

This little pig had none,

And this little pig cried, Wee-wee-wee,

wee,

All the way home.

Alfie had a little sister called Annie Rose.
Alfie's feet were quite big. Annie Rose's feet
were rather small. They were all soft and pink
underneath. Alfie knew a game he could play
with Annie Rose, counting her toes.

Annie Rose had lots of different
ways of getting around. She went
forward, crawling,

and backward, on her behind,

and she liked to slide
about very fast on her potty,

skidding around and around
on the floor and in and out
of the table legs.

Annie Rose had
some new red shoes.

She could walk in them
a little, if she was pushing
her cart or holding on to
someone's hand.

When they went out Annie Rose wore her
red shoes, and Alfie wore his old brown ones.
Mom usually helped him put them on, because
he wasn't very good at tying the laces yet.

If it had been raining, Alfie
liked to go stamping in mud
and walking through puddles,

splish, splash, SPLOSH!

Then his shoes got pretty wet.

So did his socks,

and so did his feet.

So one Saturday morning Alfie and Mom went to a big store on Main Street.

They bought a pair of shiny new yellow boots
for Alfie to wear when he went stamping in mud
and walking through puddles. Alfie was very
pleased. He carried them home himself in a
cardboard box.

When they got home, Alfie sat down
at once and unwrapped his new boots.
He put them on all by himself and
walked around in them,

stamp! stamp! stamp!

He went into the kitchen to show Mom and Dad and Annie Rose, stamping his feet all the way,

stamp! stamp! stamp!

The boots were very bright
and shiny, but they felt funny.

Alfie wanted to go out again right away. So he
put on his jacket, and Dad took his book and his
newspaper, and they went off to the park.

Alfie stamped in a lot of mud and walked through a
lot of puddles, splish, splash, SPLOSH! He frightened
some sparrows who were having a bath. He even
frightened two big ducks. They went hurrying back
to their pond, walking with their feet turned in.

Alfie looked down at his feet. They still
felt funny. They kept turning outward.
Dad was sitting on a bench. They both
looked at Alfie's feet.

Suddenly Alfie knew what was wrong!

Dad lifted Alfie onto the bench beside him and helped him to take off each boot and put it on the other foot. And when Alfie stood up again, his feet didn't feel a bit funny anymore.

After lunch Mom painted a big black R on
one of Alfie's boots and a big black L on the
other to help Alfie remember which boot was
which. The R was for Right foot and the
L was for Left foot. The black paint wore off
after a while, and the boots stopped being
new and shiny, but Alfie usually did remember
to get them on the correct feet after that.
They felt much better when he went stamping
in mud and walking through puddles.

And, of course, Annie Rose made such a fuss
about Alfie having new boots that she had to
have a pair of her own to go stamping around in
too, splish, splash, SPLOSH!

Cotuit Library

Dues for the Cotuit Library
Association, if you wish to join,
are $2.00 to 5.00 for an in-
dividual and 6.00 to 10.00 for
a family.